It's About Time
Another Place to Walk

by

Tom Firek

DORRANCE
PUBLISHING CO
EST. 1920
PITTSBURGH, PENNSYLVANIA 15238

Dorrance Publishing Co
585 Alpha Drive
Pittsburgh, PA 15238
Visit our website at *www.dorrancebookstore.com*

ISBN: 978-1-6366-1473-1
eISBN: 978-1-6366-1654-4

You will find some fortune cookies within
Slow down and uncover some Zen

Lucky Numbers
4, vi, 18, 60, 86, 88

It's my own particular rhythm I did find
Look inside yourself...it's all in your mind

Grandpa's Watch

As you hang in your mahogany case
I noticed that overnight some time has been erased
Your smile thru the reflective image belies
Ticking that causes movement of my eyes
From the glint on your crystalline face
Is that an impish grin? ... perhaps a trace

by Tom Firek

If the past becomes the future and vice versa
Has obsolescence overtaken cursive

Table of Contents

Now called Asilomar Conference Grounds was built for the YWCA from 1913 and 1929. The architect was Julia Morgan also the architect to the Hearst Castle down the coast in San Simeon whose construction was concurrent with Asilomar.

Other Places to Walk

I seek to find other places to walk
Memories and ideas tied up in my thoughts
As I journey through a collection of them
I choose one with the appropriate bent
Having seen many different places and times
I select through emotion then rhyme

Coast Trail, Pacific Grove

Another Place to Walk

It's only another place to walk
One of peace and quiet without any talk
A place to dwell on things before
And to watch the stoic centurion hawk

Remembering images of my life's lore
Things hard to forget much less ignore
As the path wanders around the seas dunes
My thoughts ebb and flow along the shore

Gentle breakers slow as memories impugn
The vision of my horizon's indistinct moon
And vastness of the ocean's shifting sublime
Brings me to realize past became present too soon

I think I'll turn around and take my time
Leaving the arriving sunset behind
To conjure new memories to stalk
By finding another place to walk

Making up games absent tactics thought through
Turning out duds while others play true
Those not pragmatically conceived
Were proofed by how many people they peeved

Having a Ball

It took the two of us a little bit of time
To procure the amount of a buck 29
For to pry it out of the old man
We had to make many trips to the trash can,
Mow the lawn, and deliver some papers
Plus controlling consumption of vanilla wafers

First we heard all about his paper route
Pulling his Radio Flyer from house to house
The first true believer in climate change
'Cause each delivery was snow, ice and rain
As we listened closely there was no doubt
For he had a weekly Shopping News route

Finally delivering he did Scrooge-fully dole
As he reached in his pocket and dug like a mole
While retrieving the proper denominations
He would lament support for the United Nations
And count the amount right to the penny
After preaching Depression stories a plenty

The purpose I guess was to lay a guilt trip
But as to our goal it didn't mean a rip
Our eyes were on a plastic bat and whiffle ball
For pitching against the house's back wall
The field we made went thru the backyard
The ball stayed in cause to hit it was hard

Whiffle balls when pitched zig-zagged all over
To make contact it took a 4 leaf clover
It didn't take long to get the hang of it
For sooner than later we began to hit
Then my brother jacked one over the fence
But there were hedges to cover the offense

I jumped over briskly avoiding observation
Hoping that the neighbor was still on a vacation
After a while the neighbor, a crabby guy
Popped through the hedges and gave the stink eye
Nothing was said but we got the message
He would keep the next one hit to the hedges

In the past he would keep balls by the score
Enough to supply a sporting goods store
This time he spoke and gave us this speech
Designed for us to be mentally reached
      "Boys as to the next ball:
    You can pitch it
    You can catch it,
    You can even Rock 'n Roll with it

     You can crunch it
     You can scrunch it
    You can go to lunch with it

     You can time it
     You can rhyme it
    You can even opine with it

     You can net it
     You can pet it
     But when it's over this fence
     Don't come and get it"

Now this speech hit us right down to the core
The need for a new game we couldn't ignore
Bro and I went our two separate ways
Grabbing my glove I went to the park to play
Champaign Park was a 5 minute walk
I would find a game or hang out and gawk

Next.............The Chase

In time games help you by becoming the means
As success with effort helps you to fulfill your dreams
Habits thus forged can surely be enough
To help you develop the right stuff

The Chase

Now let it be said on one glorious day
I beat Ruth's record and another at play
A few years before with assistance from Tresh
I uncovered my swing, new from the left
Oh the right side was working but not like the Babe's
Whose record I sought to shatter in spades

Being much younger and treated as child by all
T'was a game I worked into shagging foul balls
My earnest endeavor was appreciated by some
And I was invited to join in on the fun
I got an at bat and was pitched to by Tresh
A memory in history that lingers still fresh

He said: "Where do ya' want it, how should I pitch?"
My answer was clear and not with a hitch
'Cause ball striking to me was just not a riddle
"Knee high", I shouted, "and right down the middle"
"Keep it straight, and no curve balls for me"
"I'll knock the cover off, just wait then you'll see".

So his first pitch delivered was high and inside
I decided to wait, held, and took it in stride
"Ball one he smiled" thinking I'd work for a walk
But I was determined and a grabbed some chalk
Rubbing the bat I dug in and conveyed
"I'm here to hit" with another pitch to be made

My message was clear and he dared not diddle
For this time it came right down the middle
Knee high and straight as a challenge to me
I wasted no time and much to his glee
My connection was smooth the launch was a go
With a stroke so sweet on a trip "To Kokomo"

Rounding the bases I tripped on a bag
But undaunted was I with two more to be had
I rounded at third and being alone
With no ball in sight I still s l l l i d d d d d into home
Then Tresh did attest, with a non stop giggle
Agreed with me, my sweet spot, was knees and the middle

My first home run was had with more on the come
Thru the years I gambled with Ruth on the run

So a new summer it was that I announced with glee
"It's time to beat Ruth, whose in it with me?"
There was Bobby and Johnny and Rick and Joe
Kenny and Mike and wouldn't you know
A few others did drop out, not lacking ambition
Being right-handers all they couldn't transition

Choices of fields were found then to be plenty
For diamonds at Champaign Park, there were many
We chose a field with a short right-field perch
Which helped watching homers to limit the search
Having more than one ball was not in the cards
So not needing to search had its rewards

There was a problem, apparent to all
The fence in right field was twenty feet tall
Its height was offset by its being chain link
So we arrived at a distance with discussion succinct
Hitters must swing with a semblance of balance
While   keeping   the   plane   at   an   angle

a challenge to

Ignoring the fact that the fence had two sides
 With tennis courts being sandwiched inside
As homers would bounce on the courts here and there
We could follow their path thus relieving despair
Plus a net in the middle to stop any ball
Forgetting the bounces of an errant baseball

With no shortage of machismo and swagger to boot
Its goes without saying we were a glorious hoot
Blind to this shortcoming wasn't obvious at all
We were, by heavens, PLAYING BASEBALL!
Actors in the Holy Grail of Games
Chasing no doubt, the greatest of names

With a shortage of players and therefore some games
We allowed entry of another we called James
The name he disputed for his first name was John
But why in the world would we want more than one
Johnny you see had a unique position
Being right handed since birth but yet could transition

So Jim it would be and forever he'd listen
'Cause in that fine hour he was rechristened
Middle name first and first in the middle
He was welcomed by all with a seal in spittle
A new idea of his we all now just heard
He would chase not Ruth but righty Greenberg

This novel approach of two less than Ruth
Had a ring to us all and to tell ya the truth
Since our quest would not be troubled by him
Ya know, we kinda liked newcomer Jim
He fit right in accepting the challenge
Though first ball yet pitched was common knowledge

A child's world is spent in his own matters the most
For each morning I'd pray to the Father, Son and the Ghost
For not just success for home runs galore   p
Or the Mighty Ruth's record, but just one more   a
For you see in the day Tresh could hit 'em so deep   e
Over both tennis court fences his ball could sure   l

In truth no other hitter could make the same claim
It's that improbable quest that I chose not to name
My own secret treasure, I kept deep inside
For it was he that I chased as a matter of pride
If I could equal that feat, though admittedly closer
I knew in some years my swing I could bolster

So the first game began with the expected beginning
I hit number one out in just the first inning
A dry spell ensued a few innings later
Rick with one in the bag, hit his second 'tater
I was one behind and was pressing too hard
But I caught one inside and drove it quite far

Pulling it over the fence I hit number two
But wouldn't ya know, a tennis player too
Not a direct hit, quite lucky I think
Him standing in court one and taking a drink
It bounced one time and glanced off his shin
And boy, oh boy, did the trouble begin

The court players all, of course not our fans
With raspberries to us, we blew off their rants
The game was held up, as we got in a huddle
It was agreed one more pitch and the chase could be scuttled
The looks from court six were full of reproach
For playing doubles, was a Teacher, Lawyer, Doctor and Coach

We were summoned to court, I mean number six
The teacher and coach had us pegged, escape was nixed
With heads hanging low we approached the conclave
Our argument quite weak but with chutzpa was made
A treaty was sought, apologies accepted
For the errors of our ways we slyly repented

An agreement was key for the games must go on
So we entered discussions to arrive with detente
The teacher was straight, his case as expected was fluent
There was no room for us, if we acted as truants
The coach made his point, it was well understood
That pulling the ball wasn't too good

No need to hear the lawyer with laws to be bent
It was reckoned by us we better stop and repent
But an argument he made, court one being open
We could play ball with no rules to be broken
Though we saw errors of our ways with debate from all
We held off accepting but wanted to play ball

I argued at once that towards Ruth's record we raced
Jim threw in the fact that Hank G was his chase
The lawyer's offer repeated, this time we'd accept
He said "By the way on court one, it is tennis we expect"
"You'll have a right to a court which isn't all bad
So don't be offended, why not play tennis and be glad?"

Now this rule, with cunning, he did sneak in
We must bring, two racquets and balls in a tin
To hold court one, two guys at TENNIS must play
And a third with a glove to keep homers at bay
From their bags they gave us two back up old racquets
And chipped in, a tin of used balls and two brackets

The gesture was true and exceedingly kind
We accepted their offer with a new approach in mind
'Cause you see there was interest, to try a new game
But for some it was "no dice," as hold outs remained
For a few guys could see things, in tennis to adore
Such heresy was spoken by no fewer than four

They were Bobby, Mike, Ken then to my horror Jim
Righties them all but understandably grim
It was hard to compare topping Hammerin' Hank G
To the challenge besting Ruth's immortal sixty
So the four left with two rackets in brackets and balls in a tin
And a glove, to court one, to keep homers within

We lefties got down and started right then
For Ruths record got tougher if time might grow thin
Is was apparent by now, three were left to the chase
Johnny, Rick and myself, truly a three legged race
Yes from the left side we'd hit, which made it quite clear
Ruth would be beaten, like he played his career

With court one open and taken by the mutinous four
We started a new game with rules, not like before
This time we had one to field and another to pitch
Set batter rotations when deciding who'd hit
The at bats were even no player was gipped
So the long trek got started, with the rewritten script

The homers were mounting, as the season progressed
Rick in the lead, Johnny next, myself being last
My swing was improving and smoother it became
A thing of southpaw beauty, fluidity of motion no longer was lame
Simply a matter of time, easily convincing myself
No panic set in, enjoying a good hitters, strong mental health

As things heated up it was abundantly clear
Each homer we hit would bet met with a cheer
Not a poke to the ego a great hitter wants
But one that's delivered straight from the Bronx
For the fans being from courts two thru five
Were not supporters of, our keeping the chase yet alive

My four baggers came from something driven within
The coach was right, pulling counted, as just one more sin
I hit 'em straight into center, decidedly stronger
Enjoying the sight of a few going longer
Jim glove in hand no slue-foot was he
Dodged Bobby, Mike and Ken in fielding my spree

Once, he jumped the net, catching a dinger short of fence two
For that prodigious clout, there wasn't a Boo
The proof was there, my swing was much stronger
I couldn't resist the chance to be a hot dogger
It came in a flash, to the heights I'd soar
'Cause I was closer to beating Ruth and one more

Several days had ended and long ones to boot
Found me passing the G' man and one short of Ruth
 On this day, the next and surely the last
The four mutineers broke a few laws that were passed,
Rackets missing, 'stead gloves on hands one and all
 Did field my next blast, catching the "Tie Ball "

The "Buccos" attentions drifting, conscious way past the brink
For to court three their heads jerked, at the sight of hot pink
Head down on a ball well struck, telling no lies
The sweat rolling down went into my eyes
My best launch yet, quicker than the speed of light
With no witness left to follow the flight

The ball now gone well into the thin air
A search was started, with so much to care
Scanning high and low who'd think not far enough
It went over fence two and into some rough
The ball found by Bobby, who followed his nose
His instincts were sharp, this theory he chose:

"The crack of the bat was sharp crisp and clear,
Only once before heard, in all my career.
It was Tresh who would bast 'em with all of his might
ball cracking the barrier, of the speed of light,
So it made sense to me that   it   went   over
and would land as Tresh's that being my clue."

With games being over and life tallied true
Tresh was playing on TV with a quite famous crew
His mates the likes of Yogi, Mantle and Ford
From Allen Park he came, as the rest of our hoard
Some years later we followed in '64
And hit the ground running just like before

For the game of life we did chase
Sliding into home at the end of the race
Two Doctors, Lawyer, Teacher, Coach and the rest?
A Civic Icon and The Old Rusty Poet ruminating out West
So you see on that glorious day
I beat Ruth's record and "the other" at play.

The Old Rusty Poet

Parallels in life are just not a mystery
If one takes from the past to think history

Plato on the Move

Oh what a majestic form has he
A true visage of pomp and majesty
Shoulders square and head held erect
Exuding an aura commanding respect
Eyes of black with a piercing gaze
Rolling along in the twilight haze

His chariot propelled from behind
By an adoring personage of mankind
Moving with prominence in his world
Populated by cats, rabbits and squirrels
His bark is reserved and not one to bite
For strolling this world is to his delight

First there is Plutarch proving no friend in disguise
Likes to test the count of his feline 9 lives
Some say Plato may break his decorum
For it is hard to always ignore him
Just one short leap from his chariots perch
Could repay catty insults where it hurts

Sensing a subtle conspiracy a foot
Next he saw squirrel, Pythagorus,
    flaunting square roots
Instead of following the path a to b
He ran the hypotenuse for Plato to c

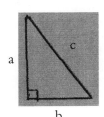

19

Now Plato's jaunts followed right angles
Not a J-walkers hypotenuse travel

$$\text{Side } a^2 + \text{Side } b^2 = c^2 \text{ Hypotenuse}$$
$$\text{square root of } c^2 = \text{length of Hypotenuse}$$

The last remaining challenge still sits
Cause he is about to cross paths with the rabbit
To one and all known as Archimedes
Who runs and runs in circles with ease
However one miscalculation with Pi
Draws scrutiny from Plato's black eyes
Which elicits this taunt from his foe
"Noli tubare circulos meos"

$$A = \pi \times r^2$$
$$C = 2 \pi r$$
$$\pi = 3.14159\ldots$$

You see Plato's world must be under control
For the laws of Mathematics to be wisely extolled
It is not an easy task for one pup
For in running the course, time is never enough
So wisely he retains his dignity
Although he sees actions in others to disagree

There are redeeming factors here to be found
Control emotions, focus, don't let things confound
For the path to success if full of distractions
Don't be swayed by others' frivolous actions

—The End—

Forward West

Things western have been a lifelong interest to me. Starting with childhood books and TV westerns, my reading adventures took me to Louis L'Amour, Zane Grey, Clarence E. Mulford, and works of everything Mark Twain. To name a few, "Roughing It," "Life on the Mississippi," and "The Celebrated Jumping Frog of Calaveras County." I had the good fortune of seeing Hal Holbrook's performance, "Mark Twain Tonight," in Sacramento, and was transfixed by every second of it, a transfiguration right down to the cigar smoke.

Earlier this year I had a conversation with my neighbor Jack, a retired English teacher and MA degree from UNR. His thesis work included much research on Twain and in turn Dan DeQuille, editor and roving reporter for The Virginia City Territorial Enterprise during the early Gold and Silver rush years. As a roving reporter, DeQuille suggested to a friend to consider writing. He hired him as a correspondent. The friend was Samuel Clemens who at the time was working with a pick and shovel in Aurora, Nevada. Initially both men were drawn to Virginia City as the point of entry into the strike it rich opportunities found in the mining business. The realization that the physical labor was beyond their expectations caused them both to find a less strenuous line of work leading to the newspaper business. Both writing styles and casual use of facts became the keystone of their reporting, delighting their readers, and selling papers.

Jack kindly shared with me his papers, notes and copies of letters that DeQuille sent home to Iowa. My immersion into that era thanks to the realism presented in those documents took me to places which I hope to share with you. I have researched, compiled and through rhyme took myself on a journey back in time.

Bodie at 8300 Feet

We left Sac Town heading East on 50
Topping off gas no time to be thrifty
On thru Nebelhorn and for heaven's sake
We needed a u-turn at Echo Lake
89 to 395, miles the least
Turning on 270 we headed due East

A journey to an historic state park
This trip was planned, it wasn't a lark
Since hearing about this town called Bodie
T'was in our plans for us to go see
An empty Ghost Town high in the Sierras
Now run by the state to preserve the era

It was just over a four hour drive
Never seen such scenery since we've been alive
Frequent stops to ponder are a must
Don't wait 'til Bodie you'll see mostly dust
The tope sheet proves it's high desert land
Above the tree line plenty rocks and sand

The road now turned into a gravel affair
It's washboard surface had our Bronco bucking in air
Now in Bodie at 8300 feet
We were exhausted, more air we did seek
The shortage of O2 left us gasping
Adjusting we found it was not everlasting

Our first stop was a must, for us to see
Making our way up to the cemetery
Graves located overlooking the town
Tombstones upright while some others were down
Engrossed reading about townspeople past
I was tapped on the shoulder and let out a gasp

For behind me was a short middle aged man
Being gregarious as anyone can
Introducing himself as Martin G
Said t'was the towns watchman he used to be
Retired when JS Cain the towns owner
Sold Bodie to the State and made him a loaner

He offered us, to act as our docent
But she was set on a Ranger event
Suggested that I with Marty should go
Then we could compare our two sets of notes
With information from both perspectives
It was better than being two detectives

So we headed down the hill then split
She to the Rangers' and us to our trip
Marty said, being a jovial guy
"Time we get a little mud in our eyes"
Not a bad idea and none too soon
We headed to the "Old Sawdust Corner Saloon"

As we entered thru the two swinging doors
At once greeted by no fewer than four
Old timers all and friends of Marty G's
Their greetings with smiles, put me at ease
They were Dolan, Miller, Murphy and Boone
Said we got there not a minute too soon

For at that moment they were out of luck
No money left having drank their last buck
I reached in my pocket grabbing a twenty
Threw it down then they looked at me funny
Why was Old Hickory staring at them
Instead of the profile of Hamilton

Snatching back their source of puzzlement
I said it must be the fault of the mint
Huh ! I wondered were they in a time warp
Or had they pulled out too many a cork
A gent playing pool came to the rescue
Yelled "Barkeep, my cover, before I miscue"

With his game over I went up to him
And gave thanks for solving the fix I was in
"You look familiar and I have a clue"
Then to me he replied, "How do ya do."
I took a long-shot completely insane
"Are you related to someone named Twain?"

With eyes getting sharp he said, " How did you know?
The time for my pen name is not yet a go"
Discretely he asked to see the twenty
"As to this date you're not from this century"
Returning his stare, I fell on the floor
He joked with the rest, " For him drinks no more. "

Helping me up, he found us a table
Straight to my face said he, "This is no fable:
Once I had a friend in your century
Who tried very hard to replicate me
He, like you, slipped into a time warp
Sought me out and I helped him move forward.

His name was HH and famously played
The exact image of me on the stage. "
Not asking for this, feeling somehow used
Thinking that Martin G. was being amused.
As I thought this, Mark Twain did concur
There's a logical reason that I wound up here

We asked Marty to join and take a seat
He brought with him a message to repeat
But I said "Before you say anymore
I would like to know just what is the score"
Assuring me his tap wasn't for fun
Getting responses was not an easy one.

Amazed I looked up and down at them both
"Am I talking to a couple of ghosts?"
He said "Well you are partially correct
Tapping your shoulder was a ghostly test
Very few respond and she and you passed
Then she let me lead you as I had asked. "

Sam said "You're like the Connecticut Yankee
We are alive and you entered our own century"
"Understood," said I, "now let's get to brass tacks
If you have a purpose why not just ask?"
Sam said, "Bodie is a struggling town
Gold is sparse the mines are closing down

We know for sure Bodie's future is bright
But that could change in a flash over night
As travelers in time we have seen history change
By going back things can be rearranged
So to move forward with resolution
We need you for our plan's execution."

"Today I talked to William E. Carder
He's the toughest man around here by far
He reminds me of the Pap of Huck Finn
Impossible to handle when drinking Gin
When sober one could reason with Huck's Pap
And Bill when dry is a likable chap."

"Bill said he'd do it for reasons his own
He would like to see this town to be grown
Recently married and had a fine wife
Who wanted to stay for the rest of her life
When she said I do, to be Mrs Carder
He promised not to drink, so much harder"

So I replied "fill me in with the plan"
I'm willing to help as much as I can."
My words were greeted with smiles all around
"T'is time we started to save this small town"
Sam said "Financial backing is shrinking"
More investors is what we are thinking."

"I have my eye on the Bunker Hill Mine
Investing in it is on the decline
Right now on the brink for money it lacks
I need both of you to cover our backs
So Marty and I could find out the score
To probe inside and to examine the ore."

So it was Sam, William, Marty and me
To create some officious pageantry
Merely a tactic to access the mine
Alone, Sam and Marty could probe it with time
To set the tone I would be an official
I said "This SSN card will be my credential"

Bill would act as my deputized agent
Keeping the mine free during our ascent
So it was Marty and I for supplies
"Sam with me on the buckboard," Bill decried
At three we'll meet in front of Boone's General Store
And get to the mine by a quarter to four

Boone did his part and supplied from his store
A miners lamp, pick axes and a bit more
Sam was missing and Bill did explain
He caught the stagecoach for Mono's last train
Destination East and out of the West
To finalize work at his printers behest

So it was Marty and me in the mine
Bill being the look out still would be fine
Of course I would be the government man
Bill taking the lead whenever he can
When we arrived riding in the buckboard
Our story rehearsed right down to the core

Bill started conversing with the foreman
Turns out that they had a lot in common
Then I spoke up and flashed him my card
A show of proof that this was not a canard
Said "T'was our purpose to grade the mine"
He replied, "You know that should work out fine

For new investors want to know for sure
Whether their money is to be secure."
Next I asked for a cart to collect some ore
He nodded "Grab one, that's what they're here for"
Marty set our lamp on the front of the cart
To make the mine adit a lot less dark

After loading our gear for the ascent
Not taking as long as would the government
We entered pushing cart number nine
Slowly at first the cart crept toward the mine
It's wheels stayed true riding on the tracks
With momentum they made a clickety-clack

Marty told me as we entered the mine
"The ore body here does not always align
Their being pinch and swell type of veins

Seams with attenuated ------$\left\{ \begin{array}{c} \\ \text{neck} \\ \\ \end{array} \right\}$------ as their mains

So you see we look for a speck on the wall
That we can probe till we expose it all

For walls there are two types to consider
One slanting out at the top / is a footer
A hanging wall slanting from the bottom \ in
Is the best chance to locate gold ore within
Look for a glint anywhere on the wall
One not obvious but hidden and small "

"When probing do not ignore galena
If it has silver it may be dull with patina
Gold will be found in strata of quartz
So use the pick axe as a matter of course
This mine has had luck with gold and silver
Each on its own can give a man shivers"

Excitedly, I found what looked like a node
I attacked with my pick for a mother lode
As the chunks fell I could see some glimmer
Veins in two directions none getting slimmer
Marty came over pushing the ore cart
Using hands and shovel while doing his part

With the cart half full or was it half empty?
We had assay samples a plenty
Thought to be pinches but when the rocks fell
The ore vein's neck looked like a huge swell
Gold fever drove us with reckless abandon
We knocked out supports blindly at random

This being a hangar type stretch of wall
Without our efforts rocks began to fall
There was no need for communication
We launched the cart with much motivation
Going downhill exiting the mine
Chased by a thunderous roar form behind

The foreman and Bill were planning goodbyes
Thinking of us with their eyes to the sky
The billow of dust was proof of that fact
But they snapped to attention hearing clickety-clacks
Coming faster and faster through the dust cloud
Were gray silhouettes, for crying out loud

Behind the cart t'was Marty and me
Coughing and snorting and happy to see
The sky once again for it was in doubt
That we could survive the cave and get out
Slaps on the backs for two dusty specters
Changed to a concern for the disaster

Sensing this Marty said with a huge grin
"Let's look at the cart and see what's within"
The ore was covered in dusty debris
"Let's go to the wash and see if you agree
That we have renewed faith in this town
Investors will come here with leaps and bounds"

With hoses we washed the dusty contents
When the foreman looked in there was no discontent
He stood there looking shocked, his mouth agape
There was no doubt this wasn't a mistake
So Marty, Bill and I returned to town
Convinced that our efforts turned fortunes around

Back at the Old Sawdust Corner Saloon
Marty set plans for returning me soon
The boys all toasted me with a drink
Pointing to the doors Marty said with a wink
"There's the portal to take you now forward
Don't be a stranger and that's my last word"

"Adios amigos", I said through the doors
The sun hit my eyes like never before
Staggering over to a sidewalk bench
I rubbed my eyes and tried to retrench
Looking up I caught site of the Ranger
Conducting his tour to a group of strangers

But there was one that I did recognize
Familiar to me by the smile in her eyes
I joined her now at the end of the event
She asked me how my afternoon was spent
I replied there's no easy answer
She queried, "Have you been mauled by a panther?"

Agreed, I must have looked a little bit shabby
Certainly not in character for Downton Abbey
So to this day looking way back in time
T'is how Bunker Hill became the Standard Hill Mine
Any mention of MG, BC, TORP and Mark Twain
Was lost in Bodie Bill's fire not to remain

Don't believe everything that you read here
It's historical fiction best read with a beer

—The End—

Out West

by Tom Firek

T'was on 16 we traveled one cool summer morn
Passing Murietta, Sloughhouse and fields of corn
For a building site we eagerly sought
Home it would be if we found the right spot
Driving thru prairie to foothills of this Western land
Passing roadsigns and markers of stories so grand

Of Father Sera, Black Bart and Bandido Joaquin
We were travelers thru time as if in a dream
Then from 16 to 49 an old Wells Fargo Route
In time past, Stagecoach drivers ejected their shouts
At lathered four horses to speedily dart
Since this road was the haunt of robber Black Bart

Teaming with critters one couldn't ignore
Coyotes, Rattlers, Pumas and Jack Rabbits galore
Grizzlies now extinct were then not defunct
But to set the mood wrong, you could count on a skunk
The cowboys all carried ammo and guns
Being low on the food chain wasn't much fun

We stopped and walked some historical sights
Of century old structures which was our delight
An empty ranch house, a one story venture,
A bunkhouse, tagged "Unsafe, Do Not Enter"
A Corral and Smithy, in arrested decay
Branding Chutes and Breaking Pens a rare sight today

My wife's turn to drive, since we did early start
Sharing this day journey we both did our part
The gentle twists and turns of 49 rocked me to sleep
For me, the end of an arduous week
Twitches and rems thanks to the man with the sand
Took me off on a journey to a Western Dream Land

In a flash it came and she was caught by surprise
By a white colored Grizzly with fire in his eyes
It looked as if we were on a collision course
No slowing down or speeding up, she couldn't reverse
Griz charged the car leaping over the hood
He stopped, looked, then ran into to the woods

The shadow he cast when going over the car
Blocked her vision, making her driving off par
With no light for sight it all turned pitch black
She went off of the road and couldn't re-track
The Bronco bucked up and down over the bumps
We were really off-roading and taking our lumps

Awakened by a splash, tossed from a bucket
Not the gentle stream, drank from a faucet
There was laughter profuse lead by a cowboy quite tall
As I found myself prone, soaking in a corral
The laughter was not of a mean spirited sort
I told myself "smile," and be a good sport

Confused and dazed I thought myself a newbie
Cast on the set of a Big Screen B Movie
Convinced of this fact I proceeded with caution
Not knowing the script, I went through the motions
Where were the cameras and the crews to record?
Action was rolling with no director on board

My dress for our trip was a casual outfit
Button-Up Levis, shirt Pendleton, the whole bit
My look fit in, dusty and gamey as any the peers'
T'was realism, with language one no longer hears
I held back some thoughts not to seem out of place
Slowly chewing my words, while scrunching my face

This approach seemed to work remarkably well
But how did I get here, was this Dantes Hell?
Then as to my wife, what happened to her?
I guess I would go with the flow until I was sure
But on second thought, if this be Dantes Hell
I'd be alone this trip, sans my best pal

A blurry state of my muddled minds eye
Joking, they called me "ta tennerfoot guy"
The group recognized my state of confusion
Passing it off as from a contusion
The tall man, Shorty said, "longer yer offin' ta hawse
Tufter he'll break, 'cause his 'tude whal git warse"

So remounting the Bronc, for the fourth time
I felt fiddle and fit to finish the ride
He was a mean one not easily subdued
Bucking, twisting and kicking, my face turning blue
With stomach flipped over and kidneys unhinging
In bucking me off, no breaks he was giving

He stopped and started, racing from pillar to post
But, it was clear my winning, mattered the most
Soon he danced, pranced, nickered and whinnied
I coo'd in his ear "I'm blue, but yo'r pretty"
So he and I sensed we should call it a draw
In accepting my offer, the ground he did paw

Breaking ones own horse was a cowboy tradition
Count one for the tenderfoot with lots of ambition
It came to me then Blue would be his name
When using this handle he didn't complain
With a no nonsense horse tried true and true
No better cayuse in the west, was Blue

Jake Sommers the foreman spoke up stating a claim
A six-shooter was needed to wear on the range
There were Bears, Pumas and Rattlers to keep from
"T'is 'bout time ya start toting a gun,
meanin' your'n pertectin' plus t'others ya see
tha Cross 40 ain't fixin' ta be a nanny"

I was outfitted at once with a Colt .45
The choice of the cowboy, for staying alive
No fooling at all, I've never shot a gun
That fact made it serious not fun
I wore the belt higher not lower on my waist
Which spoke to all, not a gunfighter's taste

Pop Upson took me where I could do no harm
At practice my first shots missed the side of the barn
He said: "Point, an' back off'n ta' trigger a bit"
Then my next shot at a tree was a direct hit
After a few hours of shooting my gun toten' skills
Improved to the point, I'd ride safe'n the hills

So Pop and I reported back to the foreman
Liking my progress he then did amend
The Cross 40 crew which needed a spotter
To ride relief as the weather got hotter
I was offered a fair and decent pay
Of 30 dollars a month 'bout a dollar a day

As the days wore on, seemed more than a few
Blue and I worked the hills, spotting the crew
I began to feel like I carried my load
My approach was humble with confidence I rode
Yet to be a cowboy much was at stake
'Til the Cross 40 finished judging my fate

At the end of the month I drew my first pay
The accounting was fair and I could see right away
Some deductions were made to go for supplies
With a bunk to sleep in and grub without flies
A cowboys life was honest, so far on the level
Must be Heaven for there was no devil

Surely my wife was in town, there I'd search
When asked by Pop, "want yur' innards unparched"
Wary of concoctions of toxins barkeeps used
An invite to the "By Gones" Saloon, I refused
A new purpose altered my main driving force
Running to the corral I found and saddled my horse

With a touch of my spurs Blue, flew like the wind
Quickly 'cause of his speed, I caught up to them
Pop bein' the greatest Square Dance caller
Was praticin' his calls while the whole crew did foller'
        "Allemande left an' Skip to ma Lou
            Swing yer gal round, an' Do Si Do too
            See Saw right, Walkin' back to tha Corner
            Then back to yer start, face'n yer pardner."

After they argued who got words wrong, keeping score
They talked of the widow clerking Miller's Store
Widow she denied, him gone, just weeks before

The answer was clear, resurrecting my life
That widowed clerk just maybe my sweet wife
I hung on the hope, my thoughts deep inside
As we entered town, it was harder to hide
We hitched up all at the "By Gones" Saloon
But I went to the store and not too soon

There was a large cowboy blocking my view
I knew it was Ike, a mean hombre too
Badgerin' the lady clerk keeping'm at bay
I tapped on his shoulder and this I did say
" 'Scuse   ME   ole Pard !
But is yer hearin' too hard"

He spun around looking down his nose at me
Said "Step outside an' whal see what whal see"
Still blocking her view she couldn't see around
By chewing and scrunching, the voice not my sound
So as a stranger I walked out with Ike on my heels
His foul breath on my neck made my skin peel

Ike was a mean cuss as everyone knows
Ridin' the brand for the X's and O's
We got in the street he hollered "Whar's yer gun"
I answered him curtly, "Fer y'all I don't need one"
Now says the Code of the West his gun he must shed
But fighting with fists he left many a man dead

His gun handlin' sloppy but his fists never quiver
Deliverin' gut punches goin' straight for the liver
He said "Look he's a pansy any'n can see"
With this I answered with much levity
For in Dojos, I learned more than to box
"Yer a yack'in galoot, ya big clumsy ox"

He bull rushed me and lead with his right
I blocked with my left and so started our fight
Outweighed me by 30 as any could see
He stood taller than I at 6 foot and 3
Being 5 foot and 10 but sure not stout
I came in at 220 at the start of our bout

Spinning left swinging my right cut back heel
It made contact with his jaw, this he did feel
He was still standing as his teeth hit the ground
But I did notice he was swaying around
Wavering he fell like a big Redwood Tree
His nose bent over, as I broke his fall with my knee

It was done for now, a fight short and sweet
My conversion to cowboy, credentials replete
Pop Upson was laughing as he re-spun this yarn
"Totin' a gun left all safe as the side of a barn"
Back in the store she could finally see
Through my scruffy beard and locks   it   was   me

She came rushing to me a reunion brief
This era was over an end we must seek
We doubled on Blue, to the Cross 40 we rode
 I gave my gun to Jake and left Pop this note;

Adios amigo t'was nice know'n yu'uns
I left with my gal fer a future not ruins
A bushwackin' fate shor'd be my plight
Fer Big Ike never'd resort to a fair fight
So I knew I'd have to drill'em
Then I'd be run down and strung like a villin
Saying bye to Blue for we had to go
To back track on 49 and find the Bronco

Now on the road by the light of a full moon
We pondered our fate and it wasn't to soon
Before we found what looked like some tracks
Running from the road and through the tall grass
Familiar to her when she left the SUV
Lay the answer to this, our strange journey

Off the road, I discovered a sight rare
Of prints in the dirt made by a large bear
Very fresh not old, could this be an omen
Somehow related to that curious moment
We saw that the tracks led into some thickets
With a large hole through these, natures pickets

Our focus was broken by an ominous sound
Back on the road, slowly I turned around
Snuffling the air was a white Grizzly Bear
On the back of my neck up stood my hair
Trying to be calm I said let's ignore'm
She looked at me and said, "Are you a moron?"

My reasoning of course lost in my fright
I said its not the time or place for a fight
So let's run like hell right toward the car
The first one to get there opens the door
She got a head start plus I lagged behind
Acting thus brave but still loosing my mind

I was picking up speed running pell mell
The Grizzly was closer, him I could smell
I saw the door open and jumped not too far
Then slammed it shut, as he went over the car
The shadow he cast made everything pitch black
Reminiscent it was from a time weeks back

I started the car as she told me to behave
Getting back on 49 this time it was paved
. . . .
As a precaution, when driving along 49
If you see a White Grizzly, keep this story in mind
So make a U turn without chancing your fate
Do it quite briskly do not hesitate.

—The End—

...on to the next, Placer Mining

Placer Mining

I. Time for a Break

Wrapping up a bid for units with lofts
Hunched over some plans doing takeoffs
The apartments totaled 200 and 20
Just one simple mistake was serious money
My brain was fried and I needed relief
Now was a good time to blow off some grief

Just out the window I found the answer
Pulling in the lot was the rep Marv's old Lancer
Products from him I had spec'd in my bidding
I would work on his prices as we were kidding
It was all back and forth, the usual stuff
He would counter me, with the expected bluff

At the window he would point out to his car
Then began his sob story that I knew by heart
Of course I could see it was not a Porsche
Then I countered and said, How is your horse?
Marv's hobby involved rodeos, no joking
On his Quarter Horse he did Tie-Down Roping

Then he smiled and finally had to agree
A hobby like his sure wasn't for free
Warehouseman Juan came up from the lobby
And joined in the talk of horses and hobbies
An old ranchero from New Mexico
Took over the warehouse a while ago

His hobby was gold panning in streams
For me a hobby was all in my dreams
All work and no play I had to admit
They both looked at me and their faces lit
Lets go this weekend, Marv with excitement exclaimed
Juan replied, On Humbug Creek is my claim

I learned to pan on the Pecos River
When the stillness of fishing made me defer
Now the excitement of working the pan
Helps me to find as much gold as I can
I staked my claim just three years ago
And have plans to work it in two weeks or so.

Now Marv's excitement was building by and by
You could tell by watching the state of his eyes
As agitation rose his eyes would cross
Albeit some motor skills might be lost.
His mouth still worked as he chattered away
Let's meet at Isabell's early Saturday.

Juan added, for gear, each bring a gold pan and shovel
We will be working sediment and gravel.
On site, for the summer I keep a sluice
Plus a small dredge to give it a boost.
The last two pieces will make it worthwhile
For three men working there's no denial"

II. Sunshine and Old Friends

Entering Isabell's Salsa Roja Cafe
I got her best stern look making my day
Between us was a mock understanding
I tease her to cause my own reprimanding
"I'll have Huevos a la Mexicana
Your Huevos Rancheros burns my mouth like a sauna.

The stare I got could've scorched my tortillas
As I ordered my special, Chorizo y Huevos Quesadillas.
My usual breakfast each time how I ordered
Declared it the best, any side of the border.
Serving she scolded, Don't touch the hot plate
My signal to eat, I could hardly wait.

The guys came in as I was mopping up
They got it to go, Guess I'm driving the truck.
Juan said, Take 65 left on 20
Then North on the way to Rough and Ready
As we get closer I'll drive on from there
More directions to gold is hard to share.

My purpose was when staking this claim
To register it with no partners to name.
I sought privacy of this lonely spot
In the past it was claim jumpers I caught.
I dealt with them to cause many hard feelings
To make their return less appealing.

When we got there we repelled down a hill
For the ventures beginning, my first thrill.
One by one we got to the bottom,
Me first, Marv next, the equipment, then Juan
We began by settling at the streams edge
Then Juan left to get, the sluice and the dredge

Marv unwrapped and strapped on a side-arm
In a serious voice, he said, Don't be alarmed
I use it when I go horse back riding
It can make the difference in surviving.
I nodded and said, I see your point
Rattlers and bears will be yours to anoint.

You can stay and play while Juan and I run
For us a choice of discretion not fun
Juan returned with his face full of sadness
Said, The equipment is gone, this is madness.
It seems the jumpers returned the favor
And came back with their unlawful behavior.

I've got an idea and know who they are
So let's grab our gear and go, it's not far.
Then we repacked our stash with an effort to save
As we three entered to move it into a cave.
Exiting we noticed the weather did change
With the sun so bright t'was like out on the range.

Looking for the rope we found it in tatters
Dry rotted and unsafe was what mattered.
Though scaling uphill was tough on aortas
Walking to town was no small "po-ta-tas."
According to Juan there was a short cut
Over rocks and ridges, will be a bit tough.

On our way I almost stepped on a rattler
A fat 5 footer looked like a real battler.
No telling who was surprised the most
The three of us or the rattler in repose.
Marv's eyes crossed as he drew out his gun
Seeing his play, Juan and I, started to run

Marv's first three shots created foot traffic
More aptly described as much havoc
After spraying shots 4 – 5 and 6
The snake knew he was in a heck of a fix
Realizing itself in mortal danger
He reversed course and took off like a laser

Things cooled down for the rest of our trek
Without incident, Marv, no longer a wreck
Rough and Ready we found full of life
For sure a Chamber of Commerce delight
Looking to us an old western convention
We guessed that was everyones intention

Juan pointed, Look, the Holy Moses Saloon
Entering I nodded to a face the room
He returned my nod and I knew just then
He no doubt was my old pard, Pop Upson
As he approached I couldn't but notice
He had a limp, and some trouble to focus.

Now "Pop" was his name not because of his age
Was given to him as a sobriquet.
As he chased the dogies eluding him
He would "pop up" in his saddle to rope them in
T'was easier to rope calf, he liked to say
In round-in' em up ah kin do it all day.

With intros for the three all around
He said, it's on me and bought us a round.
I asked discreetly what happened to him
He said last night he was jumped by 3 men.
It was a group from the X's and O's
All here to compete in a Rodeo.

Saturday's race in Downieville if lost
Will certainly come, at a huge cost.
They've been on the prowl since Volcano
Where I beat them racing in it's rodeo.
That track was 3/4 of a mile
They lost by a length but are still in denial

It's a winner take all type of contest
To supply horses for the Johnson Ranch contract.
They need horses to replenish their cavvy
By sponserin' this race they were savvy.
Me bein' the best rider for our brand
Taking me out of the race was their plan.

Now Shorty came with me for the race
A fine rider but presents too much weight.
So he stayed in Downieville to look for a rider
While I came to Rough and Ready on a flyer.
I said, Look no further for Marv's your man
He can ride better than most anyone can.

Pop looked at Marv and said with a quip,
You look like a cowpoke with that iron on your hip.
Marv said, You know how the old story goes
Better be prepared when meeting your foes.
Pop replied returning the kidding
How many notches have you been getting?

As a rejoinder Marv said, Too many to count
But to be honest an unusual amount.
So what's the horse you have in the race?
For me a dapple gray quarter horse is my taste.
Pop grinned and replied, We entered a Steeldust.
Marv beamed, For a working cowboy a must.

Then Pop grabbed his hand and said, you're my man
You know quarter horses, now here is my plan.
The race is 1 and 3/4 of a mile
Most quarter horses can't hold to that trial
They believe that, at the X's and O's
So they will hold theirs back and let ours go.

That runs Dust out, causing him to fatigue
Then at the stretch he can't hold on to the lead
But they've never seen Dust past a mile
Where he can surge faster with grace and style.
To create some interest they may have curves
To break horses stride by making them swerve.

So it's a go-stop-go kind of a race
To prove agility while changing their pace.
But speed will win in the final stretch
It's your call when to turn'm loose that's the catch.
Then Marv smiled, That's right in my wheelhouse
Dust and I, as a team, will figure it out.

III. A Rider for the Brand

Pop said let's mount, and head out for the race
So he pulled some strings, from the look on my face
And got us mounts for the Downieville ride
Then we took off in unison, stride for stride
We would be in the saddle for 6 to 8 hours
Skies were clear no worry of showers.

Now Marv being a spindly shape of man
Stuck to the saddle like he had glue on his can
As we rode along he moved like the breeze
Pop took notice, putting his mind at ease.
A true lover of horses you could tell from a mile
To see him in action, made us all smile.

When we get there Pop's plan was clear,
Juan would lead us, and he would bring up the rear.
When arriving in town we would disperse
As we peeled off, Pop would go first.
He said, Keep sight of my general direction,
To meet up with Shorty is my intention.

IV. Juan's Trail Song

We've got time to stop and make camp for a rest
'Cause tomorrow we need to be up for the test.
After dark we stopped and made a campfire
Then settled down to eat and to retire.
Juan began to sing and we all chipped in
As Marv joined with his mouth organ:

> Oh carry me back to the Old Western Trail
> To a vaqueros life of love and travail
> Cross'n the Pecos, on to Albuquerque
> Herd'n wild longhorn and dogies a'perky
> Takin' turns ridin' swings then flanks
> On to drag eat'n dust, expect'n no thanks
> By the time we get to Amarillo
> I'll be rid'n up front as Segundo
>> Yippee-kyaaa
>> Yippee-kyeee
>> Oh a vaqueros life is for me.

Trail Tune

G.T. Firek

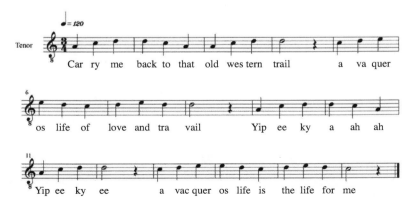

53

V. A Full Time Cowboy

When we arrived Pop went towards the corral
Then Juan with caution so no one could tell
Stationed himself at the Armory Stable
While Marv and I hitched up to enable
A one by one entrance to the Craycroft Saloon
Which wasn't busy being well before noon

Then a familiar voice said, Do ya miss ole Blue?
I replied, Hi, Shorty I'm glad to see you.
In a moment I brought him up to speed
That cowboy yonder, is the rider you need.
Marv nodded as he caught Shorty's glance
Sidled up to the table drawing looks askance.

Shorty whispered his voice soft and low
Those hombres are lookouts from the X's and O's
The way the've bin actin thar's no pritend'n
Thar' ain't a doubt, it's mayhem, thar intend'n,
Now ya two even up the score
In numbers they have advantage no more.

Their glares left Marv calm, cool and unaffected
A response that they rightly respected
No doubt he was standing his ground
Posturing like he might draw-off a few rounds
It was an unexpected exhibition
As the three twitched, with a new presupposition

This caused a change in the X's and O'sers
With their position now somewhat less rosier
Who was this cool acting customer
Steely eyed with no sign of fluster
For he was now in his own element
With nerves like rebar cast in cement

This time I noticed his eyes didn't cross
As he exerted himself as the boss.
T'was his new side that came to fruition
'Cause a full time cowboy was his ambition.
Without a doubt he let his old self go
Casting the aura of his alter ego.

The saloon cleared as they soberly left
Mounting their horses with spirits bereft.
Shorty said, Its time to catch up with Pop
The stable'n new feller Juan's our next stop.
Marv said, I'd like to meet my partner, Dust
To know each other and warm up a must.

When we got to the stable we found all three
Dust took to Marv with great affinity
Looked like a meeting of two old friends
However not difficult to comprehend
Cause the two found something no doubt about it
To join their skills in a bond symbiotic.

Juan said he rubbed Dust down with liniment
To loosen up muscles, tendons and ligaments
Marv added, I'll ride'm up the road a bit
To check his reflexes and make sure he's fit
In walk'n and ride'n him for a proper warm up
I'll get his body temp and mine to snuff.

From Shorty or Pop there is one last thing
I need to borrow a piggin' string.
A nine footer will probably do it
For me and Dust a messaging conduit
As to quirts I always leave them aside
Slaps from coil'n lasso, sets tempo and stride.

When Marv returned he thought it was odd
Seeing men on the track put him on the prod.
Posted rules say the run is straight up and back
But he saw some hombres riggin' up the track.
Stagin' groups of barrels here and there
As a straight track it doesn't compare.

He recognized a few of them too,
As the same saloon X's and O's crew.
Sure up to no good he could tell by far
They changed the track to throw riders off par.
Not see'n him and Dust observing them
Shifts the advantage back to us again.

At the last minute they changed the course
To favor their own rider and his horse,
By adding barrels for two hair pin curves
As a surprise to all to rattle some nerves.
Speaking of tricks you could see by his smile
He was unfazed and up for this trial.

"In my past life I taught barrel racing
T'is similar to calf roping and chasing
Their surprises will be to my advantage
For now the race I know how to manage.
Barrel racing as I taught my racers
Moving as one, must be second nature.

The course begins at Main Street and Pearl
Around the church where they made the first curl
Back to Main pass the St. Charles Hotel
Then on to the livery, I'll follow the smell
The mid point is Main at Saddleback then,
There's that second curl that's got my attention
It swings back, and here time could be lost
On from there to the finish line at Craycroft's."

The call came out and the racers assembled
There were five in all that slowly ambled
Toward the judge, there to set down the rules
Once heard, no complaining from those who lose.
      They were :
Pete ridin' for the X's and O's
Marv for the Cross 40 who we all know
Miner Muntz a tough looking Prussian
Pike from Missouri, and suspect in many discussions
Jack Wilson a young Paiute Shaman
Still learning the ways of life past and to come

The race Judge looked pretty mean
No doubt, a proponent of Judge Roy Bean,
For giving instructions he left out some facts
Regarding recent changes to the track
Plus another point made that was obscure
In the race it's only the usual gear.

Marv said, How about my piggin string?
The judge replied, That's not what I mean.
Marv added, How about Petes long quirt?
His reply was, It's his own horse to hurt.
Pete's game exposed could not let it go
Started blowing off steam for all to know,

I hold it thus, so I can use both ends.
Marv asked with a smirk, But not on your friends?
The return look from Pete was nonchalant
A poor imitation of a bon vivant
Marv dug further, As social graces go
Seems to be a shortage at the X's and O's.

Judge, about the changes to the course
Let's hear how it went from bad to worse.
So all can be in on the secret
For rules to be fair, square and perfect.
As a result with his game now in the open
No longer was Pete soft spoken

Losing it at Marv, Ya' cues'n me of cheat'n?
Marv just grinned like he had a canary eaten.
Now, the judge said, stop these niceties
And take your places if you please.
'Cause from the Pass the cannon will roar
And nobody breaks a second before.

Jack Wilson to Marv said, Nanatoha well done.
Now my white brother, let's have some fun.
And race for the prize Winchester '73.
It will be a good one between you and me.
Marv added, Plus for me there's Pete and our brands,
One will leave with the Johnson Ranch deal in hand.

A cowboy meets his fears every day
And deals with difficulties in his own way

VI. The Race

The echoing kaaabooooom of the cannon
Brought an explosion of hooves, dust and men
Such a flurry made it hard to tell which horse
Got the advantage of jumping out first.
As they settled down with a long way to go
The lead was between Jack and Pete from the...O's

Marv was hemmed in by Muntz and Pike
A move quite expected and to their delight
Pete set the pace but began to lay back
Looks like his plan was to stay about mid pack
Around the Church yard was the first curve
As they approached Muntz and Pike lost their nerve

Marv slapped Dust and the earth neath his hooves burned
Nose inside and his shoulders into the turn
A Marv-elous example of taking that curl
Scortchin' the first stack of the planted barrels
Pike and Muntz then fell way behind
Upped their race tempo, like they lost their minds

Smokin' up Main, Marv and Dust made up time
Settled their pace with Dust's stride looking fine
As they were pass'n the St Charles Hotel
Marv prepared his nostrils for the Livery smell
With all senses click'n he was after the leaders
To see Pete drop back he suspected the cheater

To use the second curl to take out Jack Wilson
For after the mid-point he could go for the kill and
Have enough horse left for the race stealing
By leaving Wilson and Marv's horses reeling
Closing in he reckoned Pete's intention
Since he was holding the quirt full extension

He would whip the horse to break its stride
A mixed signal in a turn no horse could abide
Marv using his piggin string as a lasso
Twirled it round and round his head and let it go
He hit the hand and quirt at the top of Petes swing
Causing Petes hand to recoil from the sting

The lasso stunned Pete and he spun around
Losing his balance he fell to the ground
Marv was so fast it was hardly perceptible
Deftly dodging the chaos not looking sus-pect-able
For confusion at the curl slowed things a bit
As the four at the turn tried not to hit

Gathering themselves they shot down the course
Leaving Pete behind looking for his horse
It was anybody's race but now only four men
Confusion at mid point was like starting again
But then Muntz and Pike had run their horses too hard
After blowing the first curl they dealt all their cards

With horses played out they couldn't hold much speed
Unlike Wilson and Marv who managed their steeds
The galloping pair of riders a site to behold
Stride for stride just like they were cut from one mold
Muntz and Pike were left behind in the Steeldust's dust
Their scheme for first crossing the line a bust

'Bout an 1/8 th of a mile to finish at Craycroft's
Exciting the crowd who couldn't get enough
From all appearances it was an even race
Incredibly, Marv and Dust picked up the pace
It was a sight for all to behold
The stuff that makes up stories to be told

Of the grey ghost horse and rider crossing the line
With Jack Wilson and his Paint two lengths behind
None was happier than the Paiute shaman
Who gave it his all to the very end
Now together cooling their horses post run
Jack Wilson to Marv said, "Nanatoha well done"

"Our tribe did a Ghost Dance one full moon before
To summon ancestors of tribal lore
In a dream I saw three emerge from a cave
One brown, two pale, as brothers they behaved.
A heeler, a seer and a brave warrior
Sent by the Spirits to stop evil doers.

Marv took it in stride, the true Cowboy Way
Acting like it was just another day
'Cause for him it wasn't false humility
In a full time cowboy's life there's no futility
Standing tall from actions of an honest man
Is an example all cowboys understand.

As he returned, Pops, Shorty, Juan and I
Greeted Marv and with excitement did decry
That Pops signed the Johnson Ranch contract
Plus Marv was wanted as the horse trainer they lacked
Pops and Shorty who knew our situation
Couldn't understand his hesitation
He said, I know in this new life I can fit
But I'm inclined to chew on it a bit.

VII. The Showdown

The ceremonies were over and awards made.
Bets were won and handsomely paid.
Juan, Shorty and Pop were big winners all
And shared in a five way split from the haul.
As for Cross 40's award of the Winchester
Pop gave to Marv for the contract clincher.

Shorty and Juan went to the stable with Dust
For Pop, Marv, and I, to grub up was a must.
Right around the corner was a cantina
Entering we were greeted by Martina
As owner and cook she was no nonsense
Her manner was curt without meaning offense

Sizing us up especially Marv head to boot
She said "You, you and definitely YOU,
Sit right down and stay out of my hair
Til I get to you don't move from your chairs.
When ordering I asked for her Son-of-a-Gun
The look she gave, made me want to run

Stew that is if you follow my drift
She replied, I know your type, looking miffed.
Pop said, "The same," as Marv choked out a "Me too"
Giving him the look she said, I know about you.
Slowly turning she sauntered away
As his head wagged in time with her sashay.

Serving up she said, No tokar el plato
Porque esta mui caliente a-mi-gos.
As she spoke she tossed her chestnut brown hair
Her eyes of gray calmly returned Marv's stare.
It was no problem to read his thoughts
As gradually his eyes started to cross.

But we needn't go further from there
As he ate his vocal skills were repaired.
It was easy to predict from that moment
What was to be his life's next installment
Though a full time cowboys life was to be his condition
Living alone was no longer his ambition

The mood changed quite suddenly
As Jack Wilson joined to share a pleasantry.
Seems Pete was taking the loss very hard
Blaming it on the trick played by Marv.
There was no mention of his intent
But from the talk it was revenge he meant.

The 4 of us left Martina's in a hurry
Rushing 'round the corner to the Armory.
We saw a cluster of 6 round the corral
Posturing, as we heard Pete yell,
There's the galoot that stole the race from me
He's gettin' his chance to meet his destiny.

Marv replied, I see you found your horse
Plus your way back from the course,
But looks like you needed help from those two.
Pointing to Muntz and Pike, new to his crew
Pete said, Oh they're members of my choir.
Then Marv, You just went from loser to liar.

With our addition of Jack the odds were the same
But we had on our side only two guns to our names.
Since Marv and Pop were the only two armed
With winks for both we went toward the barn.
As we slipped behind an empty buckboard,
Pete sneered and laughed, calling us cowards.

Marv said aloud, Pop I can take 3 or 4
I've got Pete, Muntz'n Pike, you even the score.
Hearing this, choirboys, Pike and Muntz looked lame
For you see they wanted no skin in this game.
When Pop said, It'll be a turkey shoot
The cherubs both sure wanted to scoot.

While the exchange of bons mots having begun
We slowly pushed the buckboard for momentum.
The barrier moved at a tolerable speed
Causing confusion was all we would need.
Pike and Muntz took this opportunity
To head for the hills without impunity.

Pete reached first but Marv was quick as prairie lightning
From the other's perspectives quite frightening
Bullet one caught Pete on the boot heel
All heard his "Yoweee" as he did squeal
For t'was foot to hip that he felt the stun
Dropping to one knee 'cause his leg went numb

Marv continued shooting at the feet of the three
Then Pop joined the tactic with his spree
While the hombres were doing their chorus dance
The 4 of us now took our chance
Over the top of the buckboard we went
Our eyes set on the 3 recalcitrants.

Going after the group we made quite a show
Tangling up with the three X's and O's
Jack Wilson's war hoop and our yells
Startled the dancers and we gave them hell.
A gyrating dust ball of fists, elbows and knees
Like tumble weeds caught-up in a cross breeze.

Pete outsmarted now sitting in the dust
Had boiled over and started to cuss.
Pop took charge and began his speech,
Pete, don't you think it's peace we should seek?
It's time to get back to horses and cattle
Not to see good men hurt in our battles.

Pete still shaking off his leg's numbness
Said, Ohm reddy ta call off'n this dumbness
The race'n t'was smart run, ohm given'm the nod
Jest losin' that way put me on the prod
From now on our side will play it right
As two n'aybers we ain't needn't to fight.

Pop said, We all know the proper cowboy way
So respect it will be, at work and at play.
With our energies more productive
We'll make our brands to investors more seductive
It will be to our financial benefit
Let's make this tussle the end of it.

To Marv, Pop said, You have some business undone.
'Bout time you finish your Son-of-a-Gun,
I'll pass the word on to the Johnson Ranch people
That instead of one they may get a couple
Juan said, A trainer alone is better with two
So throw my hat in as part of his crew.

Jack Wilson seeing Marv's cards playing out
Detected of him a shadow of doubt,
Nanatoha, do not worry to show yourself true
Speak from your heart is what you should do
This is my Paiute saying that's revealing.
Being yourself unveils your feelings.

VIII. It's About Time

On the first day of 1889
Wovoka a Paiute Shaman dreamt about time
For during a trance the future he glimpsed
Confirmed by an omen, a solar eclipse
In his dream:
      Ancestors would rise from the dead,
                       Buffalo return,
           and from their land,
                    Euro Americans would be shed
God's instructions for his people to this ensure
Accept American heg-em-ony for the near future,
Remain peaceful and profess their faith
And the ritual Ghost Dance they must embrace.
His prophecies and Dance spread to other tribes
But with pacifism some did not all align.

As the Ghost Dance spread throughout the plains
American and immigrant settlers complained.
The Ghost Dance was seen by them a threat
Then the Soldiers warned, this dance, will bring regrets.
In next two years Sitting Bull would no longer be
And the Ghost Dance dreams would end at Wounded Knee.

But back to the past just 10 years prior
The race at Downieville contained one outlier.
A young Paiute whose tribal name was not spoke of
Was called by his people, "The Cutter" Wo-vo-ka.
T'was their practice to hire on to ranches and farms
Using a common name would cause less alarm.

He went by Jack plus the ranchers surname
By taking this handle he heard no-one complain.
It was seasonal work at David Wilson's ranch
Here he and his fellow workers would camp
And dance taught to him by his father Ta-vi-bo
Shaman imbued and assistant to Wod-zi-wob.

Marv now suspended in dreamland courting
Pop, Shorty and Juan enjoying time, a bit boring
Left me to Jack Wilson who pursued some enlightening
I felt as being in a spot frightening.
Mixing the future past tense, could trigger reaction
Leaving no chance at all for redaction.

Sure that my words would have consequences
I decided to take the offensive

(Aside)
Please don't be annoyed by this soliloquy
T'is only from a cursory view of history

Jack, you see from the future not the past I have come.
Arriving here was not our 3's intention.

Exiting a cave along Humbug Creek
It was some claim jumpers we did seek
There was no intention to travel in time
Somehow we answered a call, not mine.
We were set out to pan for some gold
When we exited a cave our plans went on hold.

Jack said, I see you found friends met before
How often have you travelled through times door?
I replied, Enough to learn a few cowboy skills,
with adventures to bring me some thrills
and become a bit savvy to your world
and watch this country's history unfurled.

Sure it helps to look back from forward
To live and adjust as I move toward
Dealing with reasons that bring on these flights
Being true to myself and to do what is right.
The future says now things are in motion
with much to be settled from Ocean to Ocean.

The creators for change were always here
Whose approach to life was laissez faire
Until the government got involved
Control went to grifters as power devolved.
As their avarice spread and went unchecked
Distortions of humanity were scored by the peck

Morality and scruples have been forgot
Pursuits of liberties and for freedoms were fought
In our times corruption is not being controlled
And as the fate of your people unfolds
They become victims with greed on the rise
 Pork Barreled as progress in disguise.

Now Jack responded to what I had said
And shared thoughts from being well read,
I know violence will not put a stop to them
but will accelerate our persecution.
We won't accept to be sacrificed at all
to their worship of greed that creates our downfall.

In retort, As to the future, I explained
Advancing in time, very little has changed.
Good will and has come from principled women and men
As mankind profits from their accomplishments
Some evolved through altruistic bents
While others where spawned by capitalistic events,

Goodyear, Fulton, Ford, Edison, Morse
Each created their own dynamic force
Douglass, McCormick, Tubman, McCoy
Lincoln, Stowe, Thorpe, Carver, and Whitney
Ernesto, Burbank, Benson, Bell and Vince Kline
From them all this sentiment: It's About Time.

IX. Back to the Past

We ended our talk with this understanding
The future moves swiftly and response is demanding.
Change can be triggered by unlikely events
Some manmade while some others heaven sent.
There are movers, shakers, victors and actors
Cold blooded and hard, but few benefactors.

Jack questioned, How will you get back?
In reply, I answered, I have lost track.
The cave must have oracle properties
For we were moved with stunning alacrity.
Jack's retort, since It was on Humbug Creek,
There is found one cave which many shamans seek.

Wall paintings there depict shamanic journey's
As places selected for ancestors returning.
The moment you enter can be relevant
In linking you to some significant event
Or perhaps prayers engendering hope
Of bringing some clarity in helping us cope.

I can take you to your door to go back
Starting with Humbug Creek then re-track.
Have Juan and Marv made up their minds?
Will they stay and leave two century's behind
And establish a new life in the 19th century
Abandoning their lives of modern luxuries?

So the next morning at the crack of dawn
We set out to find Marv and Juan
They were staying at the St Charles Hotel
Ready to answer the breakfast bell
Marv came alone and got straight to the point
He wished to stay back and not to rejoin

The response clearly seen through our friendship
As a single man his wants were simple not endless
He grew up making his own way through life
Sometimes easy other times through strife
For this new century he had enough skills
And conveniences to him were just frills.

Then Marv said, love has found him at last
Martina and he will be up to the task
Of laying out new lives better than before
As a couple they were up to the chore
At Johnson Ranch the two would work for the brand
While carving a future with their own hands

Juan had already assigned me his claim
While Marv handled his assets much the same
'Cause he had a cousin who shared his interests
With a ranch in Lincoln and a horse boarding business
As to a hobby he became my enabler
By leaving me his quarter horse and trailer

He said, That horse loves to ride all day long,
But I flipped his name to Dust Til Dawn.
Take my saddle and all my riding things
Lastly, practice use'n the piggin' strings.
I hope you can stay with it and hustle
You've got the stuff for a rodeo buckle.

Shorty and Pop leaving passed us on their way
Knowing that I'd see them again someday
There was no need extending sappy goodbyes
Their nods and smiles were as big as the sky
Turning to me, Jack said, Let's find our mounts
Getting to the door in time is what counts.

We got to the site by late afternoon
Jack felt that it was close not a minute too soon
He said, Stay in the cave overnight,
Do not exit before dawns first light
I can't tell you exactly when to go
The spirits take over and will let you know.

There will be an event to summon you out.
    No telling how it will come about.

We found the cave as Jack predicted
Thankfully nothing hostile interdicted
Slowly I made my way into the cave
Saying goodbye to Jack with a wave
As I settled in I could hear his chants
Fainter and fainter as I fell into a trance.

Then I awakened in what seemed like minutes
Hardly enough time for my dream to finish.
I visualized a Shaman shaking his rattles
Awaking my eyes lit on the object of Marv's first battle
No need to guess when to exit the cave
Like a laser I shot then blinded by sun rays.

The door had opened as Jack alleged
Proofed by the put-putting of a dredge
As I cautiously approached the worker.
The surprise that I got was a real corker
For who did I see bent over the sluice
But Juan moving gravel in his hip boots

It seems that he wasn't surprised at all
But was killing time waiting for me to call
He said that he left a bit before
Knowing I'd arrive in a few hours or more
Familiar with the landscape along the creek
The caves location was easy to keep

As he emerged from the caves entrance
He was so happy he went into a dance
Blinded by the light he stumbled and weaved
Startling the claim jumpers by what they perceived
They must have thought the site was haunted
By the panic stricken way they responded

He took over the site and their findings
                    Then
Finally he introduced me to placer mining.

Don't be disappointed this could've been boring
Was the main reason that I was ignoring
That the swishing of gold pans and sluices
Makes it hard to get flowing adrenal juices.
Unless you hit a streak of gold nuggets
It's tough on your psyche is all I suggest.

—The End—

Where to next?

Factory Blues

My first summer out on my own
Not quite, still living at home
The old man sent me to the engine plant
Where Chrysler made 6 cylinders on the slant
He was veteran of 37 years
A legend in pistons a cut above his peers

(to be continued)

Hard Times and Silver Linings at the Mill

Next summer I hired into the Steel Mill
After testing and passing their pre-entry drill
With a shiny red helmet and brand new boots
I was sent to Zug Island forsooth
The Isle was as scenic as its name
To describe it would make some worthy refrains

The department I worked was Zug Island Labor
Sent to Cortez and on to my first caper
Riding shotgun in his big yellow truck
There to help out if things ran amuck
Sitting high on the seat set my perspective
Where we went his call, t'was not selective

Thumping along was pleasant for me
Cause breaking in new boots was pure misery
We stopped a few times and as a rule
Cortez looked up friends to shoot the bull
Catching wind of a floating craps game
For me a first, why not, it pays the same

At 3.65 an hour I could do this all day
And be up for OT if it came my way
Cortez I sensed was not an ambitious sort
The pursuit of hard work was not his sport
So I stayed with his game and kept my mouth shut
But stayed alert so I knew which side was up

When we got to Blast Furnace number 3
I found going by foot was pure agony
This furnace was down with a rebuild to be done
And Cortez said soon would end all our fun
He said "Relax, lay back, and take it easy
For a few weeks life will be kinda breezy"

We ducked and dodged around low hanging objects
On our descent into a darkening abyss
Then slowly the gloom began to dissipate
As a light appeared but a little too late
Cause I tripped over a shovel falling flat on my face
Resulting in a flurry at the lighted place

Cortez knew that he obviously blew it
By bringing in an unknown recru-it
I got up and began brushing my clothes
And was hit by a spotlight, then I froze
There I stood in my shiny new boots and helmet
Revealed as a dork but couldn't help it

I picked up the shovel trying to be cool
As one of the craps shooters said "Who is this fool"
Cortez shrank from me creating some distance
Causing me to mentally prepare self defense
Softly he said, "He's the helper on my truck"
Frowning the craps guy said, "Now we're stuck"

I ignored the banter taking no offense
Re-gaining some cool was my only defense
Slowly as Craps reached into his right boot
The crowd of bystanders started to hoot
Smooth and exaggerated movements he made
In his hand, my oh my, was a gleaming switch blade

Raising the shovel I developed a twitch
And said, " If you want some come and get it"
As my head moved scanning my opponents
I shifted allowing no circular movements
No way was I to be surrounded
Thus making the group feel any and all could be pounded

Meaning to send a message for all to see
I was ready and able to render group therapy
At that instant I saw a glint in Craps eyes
Then folding the blade much to my surprise
The knife slowly into his boot was sent
Then he grinned and smiled as a form of consent

"Well, this college kid has some sand in his craw
I can see that he will play by our laws. "
Cortez then sighed and couldn't believe it
This outcome was not how he conceived it
Craps said, "You want to rattle the bones?"
I laughed and lied "My finances are all but gone"

Then Cortez attempting conciliation
Said, "We'll find ourselves some new recreation"
Craps shrugged, "Next time don't be so crabby"
I replied, "In truth, these boots are killing me"
Then Craps said, "You can break'm in with ease
Just get yourself a can of Bear Grease. "

"Working the boots slowly you rub it in,
It will take a few times to condition them. "
In the truck I felt no sweet parting sorrow
And I told Cortez, "Let's skip this stop tomorrow".
He chuckled and was pleased that I was not angry
We both were glad this stop was not sanguinary

I soon found out that the Bear Grease worked fine
But working midnights along the shoreline
I discovered that my boots were a winner
In drawing wharf rats looking for dinner
Goes to show you that life's all compromise
Even sliver linings may contain a surprise

Please accept this as another iteration
Of a life in pursuit of syncopation

—The End—

Doing Dishes

Went to the Doctor for a spot on my nose
He said takes a minute and sprayed 'til it froze
In a couple of days it will flake off and be fine
Your nose will look good as when 29
Cosmetics aside it is a health issue
Being a place for pre-cancerous tissue

Showed him my hands rough from physical work
Not the kind you would get from being a clerk
He glanced at them and said with a wink
"I don't need to guess, it's the kitchen sink."
"It's not genetic but I see it quite often
Your problem is common to married men

So you abandon a bachelors life
Settling down to marry a great wife
Eating the fine meals as you get mothered
Her washing dishes you say don't be bothered
Doing them gladly not minding all told
The chore quickly starts to get very old

You could collect them in the dishwasher
From the table not rinsing with water
But you can't convince me it's sanitary
So you found a system on which I agree
Being stubborn about doing that chore
There's no way around it, men know the score

You became just another statistic
Of a hard headed man turned domestic
By a women who was being quite clever
Pushing and pulling all the right levers
They trick you by calling you "sugar bun"
When you'd rather live like Attila the Hun

But wait a minute wasn't he brought down
By the woman he married yet wearing her gown
It was short work she made of this pagan man
Getting off scot free fooling the whole of his clan
The pillaging hoard was never the same
I took a clever woman to break up their game."

He then showed me his own surgical hands
Proving that he was a happy married man
He said slowly not to be repeated
Mincing his words, expletives deleted.
Going on 50 years he no longer wishes
When saying I do, meant forever dishes

As a cure he gave me a shot, No, not to the head
But aiming lower on the body instead
Of steroids injected into my arm
And a prescription for salve to undo the harm
He said my hands would be clear like his
It wouldn't take long to reverse damage as is

So further to the point of this story
I wish it was one of fame and glory
My solution turned out to be simple
Not from a Doctor like Watson, but still elemental
At Costco they sell a box of 52
Of Nitrile gloves in shades of pastel blue

Newlywed, make your move do not hesitate
Be proactive by using paper plates
As for visitors use I recommend
The ones that are stiffer and do not bend
They come in prints marked on the label
To add some class to your dinner table

—The End—

Haiku brings joy
When you explore each one
Like a new found toy

Brass Tacks

In writing Haiku
The best that I can do is
Ah ah ch choo

Seeking Truth

But seriously
In stifling that sputter
The nose knows better

—The End—

One nation under God indivisible
With liberty and justice for all.

The Uncommon Man
by Tom Firek

"I do not choose to be an uncommon Man
it is my right to be uncommon ... if I can"
> Thomas Paine, "Common Sense," 1776

So who exactly are uncommon men
As I approach this subject before I begin
To this concept let us keep this in mind
And expand the definition of man to mankind
Including all genders and races in weighing
This proposition of thoughts for conveying

My age for the record is over seven decades strong
I can remember Ike's years, doesn't seem all that long
The country stood unified through worldwide endeavors
Sons and daughters and immigrants working together
Defending the America they held in esteem
T'was sweat and blood they gave for the dream

"I prefer the challenges of life to the guaranteed existence;
To the thrill of fulfillment to the state of calm Utopia"
> Thomas Paine, "Common Sense," 1776

A social bedrock for their families was laid
With unspoken purpose they unselfishly gave
To better this, the generation they spawned
Who ignored the principles and got it wrong
Instead they displayed a lack of command
Slighting the dream ignoring the uncommon man

The uncommon man broke from this generations' wastrels
Who openly pursued being unfaithful
For the uncommon man stood on his own
Supporting his dream and the land he called home
By addressing liberties others sought to disinherit
Protection of rights was fought with merit

Hence a break did occur splintering hope
Their principles refracted through a kaleidoscope
There was a thought for that, then another for this
All thoughts considered were queerly amiss
New waves of groups kept pounding our door
Replacing infants without rights, dying by the score

How in Gods name could there be a solution
To the wrongs purported in so perfect a Union
Founding Fathers sought a Republic with Constitution defined
While voices en masse supported the line
Union was formed through adversity and lament
By people wanting freedom and less government

"To think and act for myself;
To enjoy the benefits of my creations"

Thomas Paine. "Common Sense," 1776

So the uncommon man that I should see
Has his own course to follow but also must be
Supportive of anyone daring to dream
By making liberty for all openly seen
A land of fair play to compete is his creed
In choosing ones own path to achieve and succeed

Privilege and favor must be naught
Authoritarian control neither wanted nor bought
Laissez-faire levels the quest for victory
As it forged this country's history
With humanity and ethics it's roots
Elevating those in need isn't moot

"To dream and build. To fail and succeed."

Thomas Paine "Common Sense," 1776

People aligning against tyrannic oppression
Fought for the right to earn and garner possessions
United to fight for common principles
Valiantly fought against things reprehensible
Tempered through our forefathers courage
It was a united country that was uniquely forged

"I do not choose to be an uncommon man
It is my right to be uncommon... if I can"
I seek opportunity not security
Of State enforced humility and docility
I want to endeavor the risk
In personal choices not from their fist

To dream, to build, to fail to succeed
Freedom to choose anchors my creed
I prefer a life of unrelenting persistence
To that of a guaranteed subsistence
I stand with those who came centuries before
In this, my meaning of an Entrepreneur

I make no pretense that these thoughts are not the same
But a re-struck and re-kindled Thomas Paine
Done for the sake of liberties constricted
By leadership applying truths contradicted
My apologies to Paine if I circumvented
His eloquence and prose he skillfully commented

★★

—The End—